The 2023 Poetry Marathon Anthology

Edited By Blessing Omeiza Ojo

Copyright 2023. All rights reserved to the respective authors.

ISBN: 978-1-942344-09-4

Cover image by Sheila Sondik

Contents

A NAMELESS WALK THROUGH MORTALITY 9
ORDINARY, EXTRAORDINARY AND DESIGNS 25
BEING HUMAN AND MONSTERS 37
MEMORIES AND MOMENTS 53
A PLAYLIST OF LOVE AND BROKEN STRINGS 73
HOPE DEMESNE 89
SUNFLOWERS, LIGHT AND PRAYERS 99

Index of Poets 113

A Nameless Walk Through Mortality

The poems in this anthology have been selected for their aptness and deftness; however, you might be taken on a tour of humanity with the poetic languages of honor and dishonor accompanying you. So, don't rush it! Stroll gently to see the ordinary and the extraordinary as embedded in the design of this collection. Some of the words in this collection and their poetic manifestations might often nudge you into the realization that monstrosity is part of our lives. But the sane memories and moments recorded here are intense in such a way that could awaken your losses or revel memorable moments that you have had and will have.

A playlist of love and broken strings define what love is to poets and to the regular being in love with their locale. Here, optimistic poems are salvaged from wreckages and the chronicles of humanity are christened for their expansiveness and occasional invisibility. For centuries, we began the nameless walk through mortality, but because it always seems like it would start over, KV Adams writes, "Yet, we had not begun."

When we have conversations with transiency, do we forget our departed loved ones? Ellen Sollinger Walker answers with regard to her deceased mother: "I don't want to forget her." Dart Humeston sees a young persona – presumably a boy of ten – struggle to comprehend the realism of death in connection with his father's disappearance. The poet writes, "*I imagine I see him sometimes/on the street, walking briskly/…hiding his face from us/…He is gone from this world/yet his presence remains.*" Marci Darlington reiterates that "the void," of our loved ones lingers. Cindy Herndon tells us where we keep our memories: "*I have closets in my mind that hold pain, even the loss of loved ones/the anguish of those assaulted/and the torment of victims of violent crime.*"

"I have nothing left to fight for," Diana Kristine Wells writes, presumably speaking for all of us at certain times of our lives— such times when we are pushed into monstrous terrains by love, loss, anxiety, or other negative emotions where we watch a pit yet paradisiac to our soul.

Imelda Maguire uncloaks the unfair nature of the poet's experience in the poem, *The Gifts*: "*…They said/ Get well soon/but I knew what they meant.*" We find utter disappointment in those lines and the surrender to the unsparing hand of fate; but we also find the brilliance.

We cannot deny the interrelationship between politics and humanity in *Puppeteers*. Harvey Schwartz unapologetically unveils the effect of politics on us, in our society. He writes: *"we are pawns in the game/...of puppets we vote into office/...while the forces we can't control tell us what to do."*

We wonder, like Mildred Achoch, why there are "woke walls" between us and the leaders we believed knew us. In the midst of this grief, Sa'ada Isa Yahaya advises us to let our words go before us in search of solace. "Morph into a bird & tweet your grief away," she writes, even as Anjana Sen and Elizabeth Imaji Ekawu teach us the power of prayer.

But we live on even when certain things – heard or seen – "make no sense," as Daniel Aôndona writes. Don't we all have our respective telescopes with which we view things differently? We have the words to recreate our own world and define the inhabitants. Every poet in this anthology did this.

I could go on and on to mention where the poems here touched down on our nameless walk through humanity but I believe it best to leave them to your sense of discretion. Also note that in this edition, we have a shift from the usual separation into full and half marathon sections. Here we have both the full and half marathon poems intermixed in the anthology.

I honestly hope that you, the readers, nurture the mind to take a nameless walk through mortality with us. As we do, may we reach hope demesne and pick soothing flowers. May our days be blessed with light!

Blessing Omeiza Ojo

A NAMELESS WALK THROUGH MORTALITY

KV Adams
Half Marathon, Hour 18
Australia, Lyonville, Vic.

Season of the Soul

I'm driving when I see you and me like the proverbial flash
of one's life before you die. Yet we had not begun.

Front and centre we stand, then you're twelve steps behind
before you fade as you move further and further away.
Disappearing; but not completely.

Fine gossamer threads entangle us, and somehow, I know you'll
be the one who'll decide how far we will go. Two people, intersect
for a moment in this continuum called time.

The road reappears. I've navigated a bend.
You've disappeared now. Completely. But the haunting continues
like the tail end of a dream that remains on waking.

Carol Prost
Full Marathon, Hour 23
Maynard, Massachussets, USA

Coming Home

round the bend could be
anything, or nothing at all,
the cash draw— empty.

Philip Umbrino
Half Marathon, Hour 6
Mahwah, New Jersey, USA

What you are here for

Your quest is long.
Days that stretch into decades,
bones ground down from every mile.
You ride metal and flesh, sea and sky.
At the end, your eyes no longer care
to see what is at the edge of the world.
Only your thirsty heart drinks in the answer
when you peer over the side—
no turtles all the way down,
no giant's shoulders, no legendary fish.
It is the lovers, the dreamers,
the romantics, the hopeful, and other
fools who carry it on their heads
precariously and dogged.
You leap in to help.

Gopalakrishnan Prakash
Half Marathon, Hour 6
Hyderabad, India

Reality?

I was hurtling headlong into a bottomless pit
chased by dark form-shifting shadows.
A rumbling shriek of endless agony emanates
from the deepest craters of my inner being.
I come to a bone-rattling stop.
My hoodie snarls on a dying branch,
headless wonders floating on cotton candy limbs
surround me, chanting in a cacophony of voices.
An icy finger extends its gnarled touch to my heart
which by the way stopped pumping moments ago.
A haunting melody soulfully stirs my tortured soul.
A waif wrapped in an electric blue lightning
twirls in a slow-paced dance of death.
My rational brain struggles in vain to make sense,
its enmeshed gears crashing in deafening silence
What is real? What is imagined?
What is true? What is not?

Ellen Sollinger Walker
Half Marathon, Hour 8
Safety Harbor, Florida, USA

My Mother's Death

after Max Richter's piece for string ensemble "On the Nature of Daylight"

There it is again, the vibrato from violins
seeping out of my speaker. So alive, each chord
repeating like they almost can't go on.
Then comes this melody sailing over those long-bowed
chords, a pleading tune searching for remembrance,

searching for love in a war-torn landscape.
As ancient as the sun and the moon—

this dreaming, this hope of a glorious day
after such a sad night,
why do we remember things in darkness
we would never allow in daylight?

This music is a whisper in my rib cage,
a trembling in my hands. I want it to stop
but also, I never want it to stop
like you never want to forget
that person who isn't with you anymore.

I don't want to forget her but I also don't want
to remember her whole life ends so easily
with a look to the sky,
with a search for my father,
I see her smile at him; I know this with the certainty
that the sun will rise tomorrow morning.

He reaches for her hand,
and then
I see her go.

I despise this pain of remembering,
I hate these long-bowed chords
but I loathe when the music ceases
and then all that remains is silence.

Shirley Durr
Full Marathon, Hour 9
Minnesota, USA

On our Braid of the Bayou

Keeping the memory of a cinnamon sea
salted with tears and blood that are proof of life,
we tremor on our braid of the bayou.
At the elbow of the Cajun and the Creole,
where our buckets bring up more catfish than cool water—
so stagnant, its marsh gives no succor to thirsty elks.
So somnolent, its stream seems to slog nowhere.
But someday we must sleepwalk to the sea
where all water, all life flows on…

Sa'ada Isa Yahaya
Full Marathon, Hour 9
Kubwa, Abuja, Nigeria

We Might as well Become Aves & Tweet this Grief Away

Tonight,
allow me
to teach you
how to disrobe yourself.
There is beauty in this body.
We just have to learn to unlearn
our nationality, this art of wearing
a country like prayer beads. Call this poem
a prayer that isn't light enough to reach God's ears.
I have learnt to incarnate wings from broken birds,
and tweet my grief to sound serene. I mean to say I know
how to chant songs of safe flight because I have learnt to unlearn
my country. You might as well morph into a bird & tweet your grief away.

Namratha Varadharajan
Full Marathon, Hour 3
Bengaluru, India

Pluto on my Mind

After "Smell" by William Carlos Williams

I am the earth, a circle, flattened lightly at the edges,
the sun revolves around me and so do all the other planets—
only I don't know it. Or maybe I do.

I tried to snooze the bells this morning,
but was accosted, then nauseated by lavender incense instead. Ick!
Nose of mine! —what will you not smell?
the nose cannot look away from pain, nor walk away from you;
nose and me— stay around and smell the faintest things.

That day on Church Street, I sniffed, then inhaled your red deeply:
firm apples, fiery chilly, saucy pomodoro… not roses,
and not a trace of the whitewashed wall you told people you were,
and I knew… I needed to bite—
just like I knew that the one with the breath of musk
would taste like a lump of unwanted.

You could always seal your nose with your fingers—
but why wouldn't you want to know, if the stars were dying early?
Sollatuma?* —truth gets us quicker to the end.

I never exhibit words like an unfilled space, a gap,
a missing part. Instead, I say 'Lacuna'—
which needs close reading, with the possibility
of being passed over as incomprehensible.

But you probably have a stuffy nose!
Who wouldn't have known that I sit in the middle
of the universe and still feel alone—
because Pluto is not a planet anymore.

**Sollatuma*: Tamil word for "Shall I tell"

Kate McNicholas
Half Marathon, Hour 12
Blairstown, New Jersey, US

Em( )ment

After Sam Sax

The body is a temple / old house / balloon
visions of self / future / health always getting stuck in the
attic / helium / throat
and the spirits / cobwebs / voices won't let them sink down any lower

The body never arrives / dies / lives because it is already here / dead / invisible
with toes / talons / notions gripping the present / past / future
while your lightheaded skull is still stuck in yesterday / age 13 / age 16 / age 2
when you first found out about death / love / sex
and that it leaves bodies behind
You were terrified / curious / surprised enough to call
the front desk and request early / late check out

Decapitation and dissociation are the same
If you never know a body / you will never have to miss it / feel it / name it
but you can still spend an afternoon thinking about your appendix /
tonsils / spare parts
You can think of them without ever knowing them

A body can be reclaimed / reborn / renamed
You can crawl into your own / someone else's skin
feel your fingers / hands / palms spread cool gel across your / their shins
placing arnica / ice / kisses over the resulting bruises
the skin that is just one continuous organ / map / chamber
folding over to meet its own parts

Evelyn Elaine Smith
Half Marathon, Hour 6
Texas, USA

Stranded

Hemmed in by measureless cold expanse,
rimming a circular plane, pole to pole,
Flat Earther-theorists Online now advance,
a flat disk that has some climate control,
hovering above boundless depths below,
for which the fallen lack any control,
highlighting the first of all Freudian fears.

The fear of falling all felt their first year,
while a miniature sun and moon float
above land encased by an icy moat,
and stars twinkle like in a kid's drawing—
a nightmarish scene that's quite annoying.
There's no base that the earth now sits upon,
and humankind is stuck here, quite alone.

Cindy Herndon
Half Marathon, Hour 12
Maryland, USA

Closets of my Mind

I have closets in my mind that hold:
things I wasn't supposed to know about— the truth
about Santa. Or the things I wasn't supposed to do—
play with matches. Or people I shouldn't have been with
—no names will be disclosed here.

I have locked away things I wished I didn't know
or wished I hadn't seen—
the car accident that happened in front of me
and the woman lay bleeding on the road,
crying for her baby.

Or the devastation after the tornado
where parts of houses vanished
and a trampoline was on top of a tall tree.
Or after a flood where houses and cars
bobbed in rushing water.

I have closets that hold pain, even the loss of loved ones,
the anguish of those assaulted,
and the torment of victims of violent crime.

Some closets are best kept closed,
and some do need to see the light of day.

David Bruce Patterson
Full Marathon, Hour 10
Bracebridge, ON, Canada

A Tribute to Sara Teasdale Tossing Stones

The vivid autumn does not bring sadness
yet I am brokenhearted.
The cool breezes and setting sun—
those inspirations have parted.
When this season decides to end,
there is no need to care
as I see no message of wintery days
and a blizzard's icy stare.
The final peace of the golden maples
leaves fluttering goodbye,
the savory smells of my memories
are in their final fly.
Celebration clamoring all around,
giving thanks for many things— I sit,
tossing stones, imagining the fate of rings.
Carry on, dear friend
in this nameless walk through mortality.
I hear your meaningless voice
as humanities hopeless modality.

Sangita Kalarickal
Full Marathon, Hour 2
Minnesota, USA

Corporate Ladder

Ambition they say is peremptory,
make something of yourself reach a height
as if you are nothing right now,
as if you are nowhere right now.
Your history, your wins have all dissolved
into a mist and from this fog of nothingness
you reach deep in to pull out the ladder to success.
Soon there is but the image, a ladder beckoning,
no, pushing you to clamber up.
it is but a misty image
and you stare at it   stare...
                                  and there is no world,
no reality
              just the ladder
reaching high into a void.

Elizabeth Imaji Ekawu
Full Marathon, Hour 12
Kubwa-Abuja, Nigeria

Open Theory

The most beautiful things here
have a gun pointed to their heads.
This is to say that death embraces bodies
before they are given a chance to bloom.
Here, we carry prayers on our lips
and fizzle them into all of the things we do,
from the air we push into our lungs,
to the food we steal for our throats.
Lord, protect your vessels, Lord...
Here, it is sinful to ask for the cause of death,
to murmur— no matter the tragedy
that rises with the sun, learn to say praises
to our Lord—
           call our ~~hurricanes~~ —blessings,
our ~~tears~~ —comic waters.
This is the only safe theory to survive
in my country.

ORDINARY, EXTRAORDINARY AND DESIGNS

Amanda Potter
Full Marathon, Hour 23
Jacksonville, FL USA

Spacey Stanzas

I'm not of this place
I haul from different times
shifting, dimensional space
where we all use rhymes
a race for words, we create

a world, all our own
we poets of the night
click clacking on our keys
sharing stories, secrets
community through verse

Lenore Balliro
Half Marathon, Hour 7
Dartmouth, Massachusetts, USA

Extraordinary in the Ordinary

Whitman had it down, his leaf of grass
no less than the journeywork of the stars.
So it is with eggshells, their brittle calcified
cases, thin membranes lining the inside,
holding potential until it becomes actual,
or until it is stolen for someone's soufflé,
another extraordinary thing.

Shloka Shankar
Half Marathon, Hour 24
Bangalore, India

This is just me saying

feel the knot in your chest tighten.
Can you see the frayed ends?
Resist the urge to twirl them.
Focus on the knot again. Harder.
Gulp air through your piehole,
sucking in a little bit of everything
you've got to lose. It lands in your
solar plexus, reminds you of who you're
pretending to be. *Ad infinitum*.

Gail Marie
Full Marathon, Hour 24
Tennessee, USA

Birth

Streams of light trickle through a thick forest,
scattering waves in concentric circles,
rippling through the musty, muggy air.
They bathe the forest floor with a vibrating spectrum,
stirring tiny saplings to push through soil and leaves,
and make their triumphant entrance,
as their mothers shiver in the sacred
of grasping eternity.

Sandra Johnson
Full Marathon, Hour 18
Houston, Texas, USA

Haunted Home

Home
haunted—
a whisper
wafts against skin.
Tendrils white, within;
a scent mirrors death, old.
Shivering begins in mold.
A flash, something dark lay beyond—
something brittle and twisted lurks on.
Deeper, a feeling of fear hangs;
alone—the heart triple bangs.
Dread, it's covered in red;
mouth gapes, eyes awake,
a last mistake.
Your soul will
haunt this
space.

Danielle Martin
Full Marathon, Hour 17
Trinidad and Tobago

Kaleidoscope

Tripping on colors
spreading them out
watching them morph into vibrant fireworks
playing with mathematical geometry

never could I have envisioned this delight

deep hues, liquid gradients
pulsing layers of repetitive design
drowning in the magic of color
variations seemingly undefined

thank God this world isn't just black and white.

Kell Willsen
Half Marathon, Hour 2
Anglesey, North Wales

Mind the Gaps

The white walls between the artworks
Seen and unseen daily
Framing the frames
Unremarked.

The silence between the music
Coughed and whispered over
Framing the notes
Unnoticed.

The pauses between the words
Chasmic conversations
Framing meaning
Unspoken.

The stillness between the beats
Pulses echo outwards
Framing the heart
Unfelt.

The empty days in-between
Give us time to breathe
Framing our growth
Unseen.

Cinthia Albers
Full Marathon, Hour 7
Wailuku, Hawaii

Wordless

The words escape me.
They tumble around on the floor,
fly across the ceiling, wave
from outside the window.
The words are being pigheaded.
Scary. A bit too quippy.
I try to grab them
as they taunt me, laughing.
Damn— how they allude me,
scorn me.
        accentuate me.
                elongate me.
Endlessly pulling away.
I have to trap them,
lure them with sweet whispers.
Sometimes one will land.
I cannot move, I let it stay,
until others join it.
But if I move the wrong way
they fly off, or tumble around the floor.
And I am wordless once again.

Pacella Chukwuma-Eke
Full Marathon, Hour 14
Abuja, Nigeria

******, 4028

Sunrise steals my sight, gloriously;
I no longer throw stones. The light didn't creep in;
I let it sweep what was left of the night.
Here, we do not wake up to the headlines of headless bodies.
We do not take away one quarter of our dawn
to beg for the safety of our feet.
We do not pray against the foreplay of flying bullets.
We do not pray—God resides three blocks away from our home.
When boredom kicks in, we take a soft run for His door.
Here, my parents know love—every kiss taste like the first.
My insecurities are false nightmares.
My fear melts away like ice. The street is not afraid—
she has forgotten the color of blood, the blackness of pain.
Aunty Livina lives. We never die.
There is no foreign body, no tongue, no color.
My country dissolved with the night.
This newness is home.

Brian Hasson
Half Marathon, Hour 6
Derry City, Northern Ireland

Photographer

 Hours will pass before you even know it
Oh, especially in the golden hours
Try to replicate what the naked eye sees
Oh, take more than one shot of everything
Grin when you check the photos
Rain can be dangerous for the lens
Ask if you're not sure on anything
Photographers will almost help
Have fun or it'll put you off
Each photo you take has purpose
Record with your lens and the naked eye

Now read from the bottom up.

BEING HUMAN AND MONSTERS

Vidya Shankar
Full Marathon, Hour 1
Chennai, India

Stealth

(after Diana Khoi Nguyen)
is this how it found us?
the past draped about us like a cloak?

young, naïve
torturing ourselves into believing
an unworthiness that never was
stripping ourselves of lustrous fabric
so we wouldn't shine over them
shrinking our adequacies to fit into boxes
they had designed for us

small was heavy
smaller, heavier the cloak
thick warp, coarse weft
resentment, shame
resentment, shame
resentment, shame

what use is this life?

was that how cancer found us,
the past draped about us like a cloak?

Betty Jean Steinshouer
Full Marathon, Hour 13
Florida, USA

What to do

It's not all that funny when you think about it.
It's a race against time or more accurately,
a race against cancer. Stage IV.
Cholangiocarcinoma.
So, yeah, not a barrel of monkeys.
Nor a jam-packed, fun-filled day.
Just try to get things down on paper
before they blow away,
before you blow away,
but here's the clincher:
you no longer have to watch what you eat
or pretend things don't matter.
If you're shattered, just say so, or pick up
your entrails and glide away. Yes, glide!
Because when you wear all your feelings outside,
you get to emote. As in, let it all hang out.
Scream, cry, laugh hysterically at the ultrasound—
the very idea of an ultrasound.
If this weight ever falls on you, embrace it.
Make it your own.
There's no reason to be afraid.
Let it all go.

Renata Pavrey
Full Marathon, Hour 1
Mumbai, India

The Past

After Diana Khoi Nguyen

The past draped about us like a cloak,
covering up the things we wanted hidden
from prying eyes, curious glances.
Little did we know the cloak had a tear
for our former selves to gush through—
we couldn't hide anymore.

Diana Kristine Wells
Half Marathon, Hour 3
Dallas, Texas, USA

The Pit

Cold, invisible fingers wrap around my naked arms.
I try to blink away the inky veil in front of me.
I feel warm liquid crawling down my leg, onto the rocky ground.

I shift my weight, an agonizing scream ushers forth from my lungs.
It fades as it drifts toward the daylight peering in from above.

My surroundings press in around me.

The reality crushes me as I awaken my mind from unconsciousness.
He pushed me, and he left me.
The man I loved has abandoned me to a cruel end.

A romantic hike during my dream vacation, and it was all a lie.
He fooled me, and I allowed it.
And now I will die for my stupidity.

He wanted to explore somewhere no one else had been.
He talked me into following him deep into the forest.
No one comes this way. No one will find me.

A vise restricts my throat as a sob forces its way through.
I want to live. I am alive and I want to continue to live.
Hopelessness washes over me and my heart pounds in my ears.

I tilt my head toward the opening far above me.
The sun shines brightly up where life continues, but all around me is dark.
The world is unaware that I am here. I can do nothing to save myself.

As my eyes adjust to the blackness, I see the blood pooling around me.
My leg lays at an unnatural angle and pain radiates through my entire body.
I take a breath and wish it all away, but it remains unchanged.

I am growing tired now; my life oozes forth from my wounds.
The ground laps it up greedily. I cannot stop it. I am helpless.
I no longer fight against the weight of my eyelids and let them close.

I have nothing left to fight for.
I slump back against the cold wall.

All is lost. I breathe out and let the pit swallow me.

Imelda Maguire
Full Marathon, Hour 13
Donegal, Ireland

The Gifts

There was the day of three butterflies,
arriving all at once, the morning post:
one— blue satin, with shiny beads and sequins,
a twisted braid to hang it;
a brooch, gold— with white and yellow stones,
that had been sent from friend to friend,
whenever it seemed it might be needed.
I was just breaking out of my cocoon,
after my chemo, when I passed it on to Gillian.
the third— a card, glimmering orange butterfly,
the same message:
This is a time of transformation.
You will emerge.
They didn't say that. They said:
Get well soon,
but I knew what they meant.

Harvey Schwartz
Half Marathon, Hour 5
Bellingham, WA, USA

Puppeteers

suspicious muddy boot prints on
steps to a home, brazenly left
and obviously meant to be seen
because the perpetrator
wanted to throw us off
the track of what's really the score

or maybe it was someone
so oblivious that they
were just bumbling
into a heist

and maybe this
was their first, since being
so clueless you'd think
they'd have been caught

or maybe this is a metaphor
and our lives are that house

we are pawns in the game
of those pulling the strings
of puppets we vote into office
and buy our stuff from

who don't make it hard to see
their boot prints all over the labor
we've done to try to create
what we think as a better life
when they pull the strings tighter
and we can almost feel our limbs
constrict while the forces we can't
control tell us what to do.

Mildred Achoch
Half Marathon, Hour 14
Nairobi, Kenya

Cancel Culture

They used to write on your wall,
garrulous, gratuitous graffiti that made you
defy gravity and common sense.
When you began mining for common sense
and found it, and shared it,
they sentenced you to a totalitarian timeout.
You faced the now empty wall,
wondering why there were woke walls
between you and those you thought you knew,
between you and those you thought knew you.

Lee Montgomery-Hughes
Full Marathon, Hour 3
North Ayrshire, Scotland

Hearts of Stone

Like a pebble commanding the ocean, seeing
her thoughts, listening to waves and touching dreams,
the aroma of possibility fueled by the taste for solitude.
In the sourness of the color yellow,
Lee cries alone upon a Scottish shoreline
surrounded by a plethora of sun-worshippers.
Not really there— the universe is tranquility.
Hot winds, dreich days, yellow tornados of fear,
liquified sunshine held in hell. The devil quenches the fire.
This girl drops to her knees in a lifetime she is yet to experience.
She speaks without sound, shouts silently in lost whispers—
Facereius*

                      The grotesque laughs …
           You have no power here,
    in this world of chaos.

*make it right

Erica Knizhnik
Full Marathon, Hour 6
Grayslake, IL

Light it with Kerosene

My soul is a sparked match, capable of burning down
every abandoned gas station in your stereotypical hometown
that inspired every 80s movie about a guy named Brett from Chicago
rebelling against the system. The last bit of the pungent,
addicting smell of gas left in one of the barrels
is enough to light the world in the darkness of dawn,
a warm glow recreating a painting of orange and yellow swirls
with the charred taste of revenge as everything goes *Boom*.
But my burnt match of a soul has difficulty sparking anything in life
when floods of thinking sizzle out the last of the smoke
and the world is washed over in gray.

The sky is a clear blue, early morning birds chirping over an empty lot,
their wings flapping away the fires where its passionate life stood
minutes before.
The motionless air brings about the sadness of reality that there is
nothing left
of the past or present or the time anything ever mattered in the first place.
The fertile land will always be covered in nothingness, dried up flowers
packing their bags and flying off into the sunset,
a shooting star that will never rise again.

The burning fire is cold and heartless in her darkened hands
covered in potassium chlorate, sulfur, fillers, and glass powder,
the same material that gave life to the glowing match;
"Tutto è bene ciòchefinisce bene".
But now, the station will forever be on fire.

Diane O'Neill
Full Marathon, Hour 16
Chicago, Illinois, US

How to Create a Great Nation

Teach children love-your-country tales,
forget boring dates and facts. Keep it upbeat!
If you have to mention mistakes, find positives
in genocide, slavery, and oppression.
Be creative— you can do it!

If libraries insist on sharing truth, go after librarians.
If people threaten violence, wear earplugs.
Proclaim your Christianity—but YOU know
that blessed be the Rich and the Warmakers.

Forget the *love thy neighbor* stuff when it comes
to people who are different. Cite obscure dogma
when trans people seek rights.
Ban any books that suggest love is love.
Don't dare let kids read about two penguin dads!

Keep migrants out.
That "Give me your huddled masses" sentiment
is just a poem on a statue.
Never look in a mirror; what you see might scare you.

Stephanie Ross
Half Marathon, Hour 11
Courtenay, BC, Canada

Gongjing

Gongjing* fabric of the Universe

    held in a baby's palm
    whispered in first words
    shining brightly from innocent eyes

Gongjing movement in the exchange

    suckling mama's milk
    heart beats in unison
    love at first sight

Gongjing birthing new horizon

    orange waves across the mountains
    eternal sunrise flying eastbound
    flatwater calm beyond my vision

Gongjing rising within me

    dissolving into everything
    expanding into nothingness
    knowing myself for the first time

*unity, oneness, deferential respect

Ofuma Agali
Full Marathon, Hour 4
Lagos, Nigeria

The Season of Prayers

They are burying
their witless open secrets
in void orisons

They are seeking the
faces of supplication
merchants, in vacuums

They are plucking out
stars from the dark skies, sweating
All wide eyes on them

They are exhuming
their decayed consciences from
graves of opulence

They are sending scared
sacrifices to a heaven
that will not open…

Daphne Joy Grant
Half Marathon, Hour 14
Mission Viejo, California, USA

Sisters Beside Us

From birth we age
in labored groan—
from youth to sage,
from babe to crone.

Sisters beside us
women never alone—
from ashes to ashes,
to dust and bone.

Sue Storts
Half Marathon, Hour 9
Tulsa, OK, USA

Grateful

Lovely mid-summer Colorado day
overflows with flowering baskets overhead.
Little blond girl dances in pink snow boots.
Tables of people break out in uproarious laughter.
Large, happy families eat burgers, drink local brew,
joyously swallow life, enjoy patio time together.
As I smile, my so-grateful mind leaves my body
behind. I choke on vague uneasiness
as I approach the age at which my mother died.
Bones and muscles wonder
what might come next to take us all out.
I catch my shallow breath,
shoulders near my ears.

MEMORIES AND MOMENTS

Dart Humeston
Half Marathon, Hour 2
Lake Placid, Florida, USA

Ten Years Old

Dad has been dead for two years now
as my ten-year-old brain
struggles to understand
what death is.
I imagine I see him sometimes
on the street, walking briskly
carrying a folded newspaper,
hiding his face from us.
Why did he leave us?
Something I did?
My little brain can barely
comprehend life,
let alone death?
Dying?
What the hell is that?
He's gone, and two years later
I still can't understand why.

I still feel his unshaven cheeks
scratching me when he hugs me,
his eyes smiling into mine.
He is gone from this world
yet his presence remains.
Hints of another life
another existence
beyond my
understanding.

Britton Gildersleeve
Half Marathon, Hour 3
Blacksburg, VA

Death is a Fallow Field

Memory what grows there, thin and fragile-stalked
fragrant as basil, a cacophony of birds.
I can taste their songs; honey on the tongue.
Glen told me once, perhaps on a boat floating down
an ancient river, one of so many we rode together
that death was a killing field.

Nothing grows there, he said. But I have seen the leaves
sway beneath the Lahaina banyan and maybe it will live.
Perhaps the fire ignited a phoenix heart
nestled among those thousand trunks, the igneous gold
of survival where fire becomes wings
and I can fly to you on bright feathers.

Britt, he told me, I am leaving.
Welcome death for me. It is my friend.
Non, I answer: *Le mort n'est pas notre ami.*
The banyan tree nods its many naked, seared heads
and the fallow field of death nods too,
lightly furred with green.

Tanya Gogo
Full Marathon, Hour 1
Hoquiam, Washington, USA

Orphan's Dilemma

Surrounded by boxes and bins,
the weight of yesterday
shrouds me in memories and guilt.
It gnaws at me.

But I can't keep you all,
I think.

Even years later,
I have to remind myself
that I can't make space
for the future draped in relics.

I wrap myself in the memories,
release the guilt,
take a deep breath,
and let one more piece go.

Marci Darlington
Half Marathon, Hour 8
Mt. Sterling, Ohio, USA

Called up to the Big League

For Lori who played over 50 Women's Softball League.
She died of brain tumor.

She knew how the game was played
and the role she would play in it.
She was a competitor not to be overlooked
even on the days when her fiercest opponent
would beat her down. Her strength and confidence
were soothing to those of us questioning what we knew to be
she would be called up to the big league
for they had scouted her since 2021.

Her journeys with the team took her away from home
but she would always return with stories of winning hits,
great times with teammates, even a broken nose.
Her last game here would not disappoint
as she hit the game winning RBI,
clinching the National Championship for her team.

But with all the cheers and way-to-go's
came the somber realization
the big league wanted her, it was her time now
and so, she left us.

It has been over five months,
the void from her absence lingers
and challenges our beliefs, but we are blessed
with our memories of games and gatherings,
the warmth in our hearts for knowing her,
and the honor of calling her our friend.

Pamela Gerber
Full Marathon, Hour 5
Huntington Beach, California, USA

Verity

Where did you go, my long-lost friend?
Growing up, I learned from my mother
who sang your virtues, triumphs, and worth.
She called you holy or whole or simple.
Ever elusive— you, an abstract idea
invested in me, the guilty vestibule,
and once piqued a guardian embarrassment,
a red-faced heat before honed stares.

A Google search bore nothing,
mere letters, dancing 1s and 0s, but not you,
my once hero-now-gone-missing-sister,
a wife to wicked hissing serpent sins.
Last seen among the silent ones—
a mute testimony and vibrational grasping.
You whose innards sparkling clear waters to wind,
I miss you, motionless, paralyzed by lies.

Jo Eckler
Half Marathon, Hour 9
Austin, Texas, USA

Echoes

The first tremors of cold
have me pulling on the jacket you left behind
(along with everything else)
The bayou fades as I drive
Elbow propped on the window frame
(Like you used to)
There was that time we paused,
panting beet-red from hiking
That elk's deep eyes meeting ours
in holy communion
(Now I alone remember)
The lightbulb in the carport flickers out as I pull in
I add it to the grocery list, right after cinnamon
(And wish you were here to change it)

SincerelyBlueJay
Full Marathon, Hour 16
Las Vegas, Nevada

September Whispers your Name

Remember when we would go to the nursing home
and glue puzzles together and trade books worn out
and weighed down with the annotations of
literal generations – we painted sunflowers
and lilies for each room with a little old lady lacking
family or support. We made such a routine out
of being there to name the hummingbirds whenever
we lost someone to the garden and chasing fireflies
for the old men in walkers still in love with the
dream versions of their wives and kids—already passed.

I don't know why the smell of pine sol and lemon
are so distinct to me when the memories were
actually so bright and the lessons that were
inherited within those walls so valuable—I don't know

why I can write poems for Shirely's mom
but when I want to write for Shirley herself or
mourn Johnny (I'm late to that party too) the pen
just dries up so completely it can't be salvaged
and the computer freezes and the internet dies
and the storm drags all my ideas to a city that
will never appreciate them the way I did.

Her birthday is coming up soon and she hasn't
returned my calls for the last two years, but
I'll go ahead and give her a ring anyway.

Wouldn't you?

Karen B. Call
Half Marathon, Hour 9
Aurora, Colorado, United States

Keeping Secrets

The bright light illuminated the bucket
in the corner of the carport. Dusty fishing poles
stood in it, ready. An elk, one of the few
in the area, stood just outside the light ring,
head tilted. The smell of cinnamon
wafted out the window and drifted
into the air.

He pulled his jacket from the hook—
time to go feed the animals.
He turned away from Alice and picked up
the remains of their dinner. His hand shook.
The tremor was increasing. How long
before she saw it? He grasped his arm,
opened the door and walked
into the summer evening.

Tears made tracks over her cheeks
as Alice watched him.

Leroy Leonard
Half Marathon, Hour 1
Centennial, Colorado, USA

Eight Years Old

Frozen in a candy store
at eight years old

Aromas of cherry
and licorice

Wrap around me
like a corset

I'm crushed
in an avalanche

A flood of colors
a cascade of chocolate

This deluge
this ocean

This bottomless
pit of possibilities

While my sister
gently without hesitation

Cinderella-esque
chooses just one

Steps to the register
her eyes neither right nor left

And I feel like shit
while my mother says

Hurry up, Leroy
there are people behind you

David L. Wilson
Full Marathon, Hour 2
Wailuku, Hawaii, USA

65 Years Ago

Back when the pants she wore were called dungarees,
the tomboy and I roughhoused in the backyard at Bradley's house
where a trellis produced white roses you could eat, so I was told.
I had suspected a trick but they tasted sweet.
Amid the grappling and grunting,
suddenly, a mystery scent arose—
an odd presence reached from the soil beneath us,
puzzling the space surrounding us.
We stopped, looked at each other and moved apart.
We didn't wrestle again.

Daryl Curnow
Half Marathon, Hour 8
Auckland, New Zealand

Brighter Horizons

The silhouetted strings play over my heart
casting a buoyant shadow
that better things are to come
a brighter horizon

Like the climactic scene of a film
it's building to something
something purposeful
something worth holding on to

It could be a soft kiss
a warm hug
a gentle smile
sometimes that's all it takes

to get through

As the cellos echo out
in my orchestra of life
I appreciate the little things
I appreciate you

It's not validation I seek
it's belonging
in your world
and in mine

in ours

I let the subtle notes sink in
to lift my body above the ground
I'm soaring so high

and it's beautiful

Ipsita Banerjee
Full Marathon, Hour 22
Kolkata, India

Pizza

We were never alike in many ways
but we managed a semblance
of common ground, at least where it counts.
I like spinach and Ricotta cheese
with buttered garlic sprinkled on top
while you have your pepperoni
steaming hot, straight from the box.
Will you meet me halfway, where the picnic tables
jostle the weeds against a Tuscan sky?
You bring the Pinot Grigio,
I will pack the chequered blanket
and we can sling away the sunset,
and brave the seven seas once more!

Aarthi V. Karanam
Full Marathon, Hour 1
Mumbai, India

Timeless Love

We stood under the moonlight,
the birch throwing about strange shadows.
Our shadows got lost in them.
Or did we become one ourselves?
A truant breeze slapped against our faces,
our hands entwined and we simply walked.
The leaves sighed, the wind whispered
and our past murmured the stories of our smiles,
our love, of battles we fought and lost…
Time marched on, the world changed,
so did our bodies and faces.
But today, under the cloak of the stars,
as they whispered secrets deep, we traced our history
amongst the shriveled-up roots of trees
and the fading hush of the night sky.
In each other's arms, we sketched the journey
of our several lifetimes and time stood still
for an infinitesimal moment, peering at us,
soul to soul, soul over soul, soul with soul.
And this is how she found us,
the past draped about us like a cloak.

Stefanie Hutcheson
Half Marathon, Hour 8
NC, USA

Songs Remember When

Faded photographs of album covers flit across the television screen
as songs from my past are harmonized by those I once crooned along with.
The *Hollies* sing of my brother not being heavy and I'm there, remembering Billy.
Moments ago, it was the Marmalade, singing *Reflections of My Mind*.
As I recalled how I used to think the chorus said *Take me back to my Momma*.

Remember Elton John's one about diamonds?
I thought he sang *Put me in the sky with God* as I'd twirl around in the yard.
America sang about needing someone like the flowers needed the rain
and I remembered one night playing Solitaire and murmuring, I need you
to my unrequited love. When a few moments ago Elvis sang
about his suspicious mind, I remembered a deejay once saying
how he loved that song because it allowed him to take
an extra-long bathroom break when another chorus faded in
to rile up the lovers again.

Now Neil Diamond is singing *Play Me*.
I took that one to heart–but got played instead.

Let's move on.

Oh great: more Elvis, singing about that rain in Kentucky.
How I used to yearn for someone to seek me out like that.
Ahh, there's Carole King with songs from her Tapestry album.
For some reason, that one makes me think about life as a kid in California.
Each time I hear *The Sounds of Silence*, I remember the melancholy.
No matter what is going on, I must stop what I am doing
and pay due homage to that classic. The nearly maniacal laughter
in the *Guess Who's* song makes me question my own madness.
Are you laughing at me now?

Gordon, if you could read my mind, could you make sense of this?
That was another favorite that takes me back to my life as a young one
without a clue. And now, we're to Nilsson and his heartbreaking ditty
about not being able to live if living is without you.
That one makes me think about you. You know who you are.

All of these songs have been played since the start of this poem.
Ironic, since they probably started off as poetry themselves.
Songs worth a thousand words but narrowed down to few stanzas.
A few lines that encompass my life— or at least a large part of it.

Music: a word picture that we all hear in different ways, conflicting lights, and yet bringing us all together and making us see.

Diane Carmony
Half Marathon, Hour 3
La Quinta, California, USA

Morning Songs

A crow calls, celebrating the morning.
I listen closely to chronicle
the answered greetings
of the chestnut-backed chickadees.
Soon others join in:
a Steller's jay, a brown creeper,
now the barn swallows
and a red crossbill.
A squirrel adds his shrill chirping.
I sip my coffee and peer up
through the branches of towering firs,
into the cloudless blue sky.
I am untethered, free.
The leaves rustle in the wind,
dogs bark today's messages
and far-away voices catch in the breeze.
In the distance, I hear the waves:
the ocean beckons.

Pamela Salmon
Half Marathon, Hour 4
New Jersey, USA

On The First Day of Spring

I drove by that place you took me once
because your father was still building
those beautiful houses
that were only bones of themselves.
We could only see the darkness
that laid between the framed wood.
It filled our imaginations with delight
and so we parked and kissed deeply.
Now those moments are etched
in our hearts like matching tattoos
or the stained-glass windows on the finished house
that even your mother's strident disapproval
couldn't remove. I want to share this with you
as the sun melts the snow and leaves.
The crocuses are blissfully naked and dripping.
This is the moment I chose for you
to relive with me now
as it should have been then.

Bonnie Katzive
Half Marathon, Hour 12
Boulder, CO

Housecleaning

I cleaned my closet last week,
the one where I keep our unfinished business
and poorly analyzed memories.
I found timelines twisted and knotted
inside boxes like old yarn—
the old book I made for your birthday,
the invitation the children wrote
for a stuffed animal wedding,
the knight costume I made for Halloween,
a worn-out tee shirt I can't bear to throw away,
old spinning tops that made my mind spin
out sweet moments. I took it all out, sorted it,
returned each item to its box
until time comes to clean again.

A PLAYLIST OF LOVE AND BROKEN STRINGS

Daniel Aôndona
Full Marathon, Hour 10
Abuja, Nigeria

What Love is to a Broken Poet

My pen dances to the rhythms of grief
like a mighty cow trampling the field for green food.
I hold its tip, each drop of ink is a dedication
to the unfading scars hung on my flesh.
Just then, a lassie walks majestically into my life
singing a strange song, love lyrical.
She attempts to steal away my already locked heart
conning me with a romantic accent which my heart
pays no attention to. She subtitles her love language,
preaching hard to convert my soul. Her sermon
makes no sense to me because in my own story,
love is an outcast with a pungent smell.
She is unwanted— her presence stinks away my sanity.
In my heart, I strike out the letters that spell love
because love is nothing but the epitome of grief.

Mary Eugene Flores
Full Marathon, Hour 10
Manila, Philippines

What is Love?

Love is something that I'm afraid to try
despite the ambrosial temptation behind every word.
A romantic action or a feeling,
a limerence aftermath,
after a deep conversation,
or an eye-to-eye contact.

Love— something I doubt my whole life.
It's like a turbid ebb of reality slapping you back and forth.
It left you a red mark on your face,
It left you hanging, less breathing after a race, traceless.
Love kept you running, without even moving.

Love? It's a hoax serendipity,
throwing a coin on a fountain,
or meeting a guy on a train—
such random acts won't last a lifetime.
What else would've persisted?
If not love? What is it?
What is love?

Katrina Moinet
Half Marathon, Hour 12
Llanfairpwllgwygyll, Wales

Vivisection

I think of you daily, which is not to say fondly.
I'm waiting for that memory to return
the one that confirms you a monster and I,
more vulnerable than I'd care to remember.

What is it to love a person who wronged you
other than a reconditioned love?
Disclosure implies letting go, a confession:
how was I to know I'd allocated you
a tiny square inside my heart.

Dissection suggests some swift separation
cleanly halved, and yet I've found it
far more jagged, less deliberate.

You know, when one door closes
another trauma opens.

Bhasha Dwivedi
Full Marathon, Hour 14
Lucknow, India

What is Love?

What is love if not a poem
written, spoken, expressed, hidden?

What is love if not a story
told, heard, repeated, forgotten?

What is love if not a song
hummed, sung, played, faded?

What is love if not a picture
drawn, admired, appreciated, torn?

What is love if not your presence
there, needed, neglected, gone?

What is love if not regret
felt, kept, revisited, locked?

What is love if not you and I
there, together, staying, forever?

Michelle Adegboro
Full Marathon, Hour 2
Abuja, Nigeria

Atavistic Memory

I riffle underneath the image of a child counting 5 on her palms,
I want to exhale the alternate of a dark desire in a dream that is not mine.

//

In the telescope, I see the stars in black shades, up-down.
My desire is to clutch you in my arms & watch the white board
with images of relics— an eclipse of reaching heaven.

//

I'm in the 5th
& I still wander in the shadows of dark paintings.
I see images of waking wounds with a girl standing on her feet.

Tim Spadoni
Full Marathon, Hour 10
Pingree Grove, Illinois, USA

What is Love?

we walk in the woods
warming our fingers with touch
the cold disappears

Amber L. Crabtree
Full Marathon, Hour
Mesa, Arizona, USA

If I Could Go Back to When Things Were Perfect

We'd still wake up
next to each other in the mornings.

You'd make me tea
while I watch you adoringly.

Every move you make
as perfect as the one before.

I'd still think you were sent to me
to teach me how to love, again.

Amy Bostelman
Half Marathon, Hour 10
Leander, Texas, USA

Fairytale Love

What love is—
not Cinderella and the glass slipper

Rather it's slipping on the glass
then given a hand to stand up;

What love is—
not Sleeping Beauty awakened by the kiss of a century

Rather it's breakfast in bed
after sleeping in on Sunday morning;

What love is—
not Belle dancing at the ball with a kind atrocious Beast

Rather it's permission to miss the ball
and cuddle with that kind atrocious Beast;

What love is—
not being awakened with a kiss after biting into poisoned apples

Rather it's being loved enough
for a back slap to dislodge the apple pieces;

Love is Living the Real Life—

with all of the slips and falls;
sleeping through mornings;
staying home for the night;
and rescues from unruly apple chunks.

Liane Sousa
Half Marathon, Hour 1
California, USA

Missed Love

After Diana Khoi Nguyen

At an elegant dinner in a restaurant
we used to only dream about,
we began to reminisce over a glass of wine.

He started with our first date
four decades ago, and how we drove
to an isolated country road
and danced in the moonlight, swaying
to music drifting from his truck's radio.

I recalled the Christmas tree adventure
when he brought his own lumberjack axe
and chopped down an enormous noble fir tree
that barely fit in the truck.

We remembered how we met at a three-hour
night class at a community college
and bonded over lecture breaks,
and how he would meet me for lunch
when I was working.

Our eyes locked while we laughed,
remembering fun times that were sprinkled
with magic dust…each knowing that if the timing
had been more aligned, our life courses
would have been different.

The restaurant melted away as we
engaged with our warm memories…
This is how she found us—
the past draped about us like a cloak.

Sandra Duncan
Full Marathon, Hour 18
Portland, Victoria, Australia

Morning Memories

I feel your breath in my hair
In my empty bed
In my room

Your scent reaches from beyond
A mix of hunger
Rose and mint

Crawling up my nostrils
Into my memory
Pulling tears

Dreams and nightmares crowd my body
My heart thumping
Senses strung on nerves

Waiting for you to appear

Katarzyna Stomska
Full Marathon, Hour 15
Kilmarnock, Scotland, UK

Long Gone

Long gone are the days—
us holding a heartfelt thank you

Long gone are the moments
of innocent hugging of bodies

Long gone are the minutes
our breaths blended in an instant

Long gone are the adventures
excitement changed into shame

Long gone are the feelings of love and unity
—all that's left is an empty space

Margarette Wahl
Full Marathon, Hour 23
Massapequa, New York

A Montauket Sunset

A summer day draws towards a close.
At a Montauk bar, the Montauket named with a hotel
after a Native tribe, bar staff wear natives on their t-shirt backs
as they serve frozen mudslides that slide down cool and smooth
after a day of August heat.
                        Next comes a sunset like no other,
where crowds line up to get a grand view.
This Eastern end sky turns orange, lavender, pink mixed with blue.
As quick as this change takes form, the sun bows lower and lower
into a gradual transition towards the water edge,
past the ground, until it's eventually swallowed up and disappears.
This place is like heaven in its beauty of painted sky.
Sometimes, it feels like a different world—
a world away especially without you inside it.

Cynthia Hernandez
Full Marathon, Hour 19
Bremerton, Washington, USA

Past Midnight

Moon glow casts shadows
on the closet door—
geometric watercolors that flicker.
I watch them for a while
before turning toward the window
and the grace of your bare arm:
a luminous silhouette.

My gaze travels along the smooth
and curve of you,
and finally rests on
the leg you've flung over the duvet,
toe pointing toward morning.

Fortune Simeon
Full Marathon, Hour 3
Abuja, Nigeria

A Country is a Playlist of Broken Strings

"...one mind dey tell me to disappear..." from Omah Lay's Soso

I whisper afrobeat into a body
full of wa(te)r to see how far it filters
loneliness from hope.
Here, everything dissolves in music—
love, war, art & blood.
So, this art is a cauldron of enjambed imagery
dissolving in broken strings, into soprano,
into a country. Here, blood is trademarked
on the soil beneath my country.
And beyond this broken playlist, I long
to ask *Omah Lay* how much pain
Soso can take away—
if a deceased country could also fit in.

HOPE DEMESNE

Shaughnessy Andrew
Half Marathon, Hour 4
Toronto, Onatorio, Canada

Little White Chapel

In my heart, there are four rows of pews,
empty, these simple planks, hewn
from wood salvaged from a wreckage,
fastened with nails left unused

from what should have been a lifetime
of building. The altar table has been austere
since it stopped holding wine, which is fine
since there has not been a service

in the chapel of my heart since you said
it would be a cold day in hell before you
fell in love with a heartless wretch.
I'm hoping you got part of that wrong

Maria Riofrio
Half Marathon, Hour 6
New York, USA

If the Earth Was Flat

Will you meet me
at the edge of the world?
Two halves of a whole
hanging on for dear life.

Memories—aching to breathe
are released. Some are stones,
others become butterflies.
We don't get to choose their trajectory aloft
or in free fall.

I sing and there are no echoes.
The sound takes a nosedive
and might be captured by a comet
just passing through,
setting its tail to music.

I reach out my hand—
and if you grab it from beneath the
precipice, I know there is still hope, maybe
even love though that can plummet too;
always a boulder and never a feather.

Mardiosa Yañez (HighEarth8888)
Full Marathon, Hour 9
Manila, Philippines

Hope Amid the Pain

A shiver speaks amid the vacuum, a voice that echoes in the dark.
It lifts me up from the fragments of pain, to challenge the foible within,

to find the spirit that shakes my soul. It ushers me to the lightbulb
that flickers in the distance, the lightbulb that flickers.

The lightbulb that flickers is the touch of love, gentle
and soothing on my wounded spirit.

It guides me through the woods like an elk, graceful and alert.
It ushers me to a space where dreams awaken, where possibilities unfold.

It shows me the beauty of the earth, despite the moonless night's blues.
It shows me the lightbulb that flickers.

The lightbulb that flickers is the strength of hope, enduring and resilient in my heart.
It bears all things that come my way, all tumult and sadness that worry me.

It reassures me with its existence, with its warmth and glow.
It expels the fear and doubt I feel, it fills me with confidence and faith,

It draws me to the calming lightbulb, the lightbulb that flickers.
The lightbulb that flickers is the spark of life, priceless and blessed in my being.

It shines through my flaws and imperfections, through my cracks and scars.
It reveals my inner self, my substance and purpose.

It invites me to embrace it, to caress with it.
It calls me. It calls me to watch the lightbulb that flickers.

Anna Markowitz
Half Marathon, Hour 7
Los Angeles, California

Conversion

my mother worships a god of parking spots.
all the problems and all the wars
and all those hungry babies—
but i do the easy things first, too,
cross off wake up, make coffee, on a list
that might go on to cure cancer
or walk the moon— but probably not.

life is discovery, i guess,
every pathetic love letter, every dew-fresh morning.
and why can't they live together,
that old witch and her goldfish,
why not every odd pairing,
every gift given freely, every city swinging wildly
on the grand dumb whim of tectonic plates?

i don't want your white-lined,
sanitized, god of convenience—
don't ask me to pray.
instead, i'll believe in:

a caught breath, the pause before,
every wish i have for you,
every wringing hand.
the last croak of the percolator,
the welcoming dawn.

sure as that first awareness
of the damn cat outside and the sun on the window,
today's another knock-down, drag-out, fifty-fifty,
and tomorrow is the place
where i gently plant my hope.

Ayah April Soliman
Full Marathon, Hour 24
Saltspring Island, BC

Hope

I lost you somewhere along the way,
amidst the shadows of those dark days.
I slipped you out of my heart,
and traveled far away from you.

I lost you somewhere along the way.
My path, full of thorns and broad turns.
I know you are there somewhere.
I feel you when my mind is serene,
when I'm plugged into God's Grace,
on a sunny Sunday afternoon.

I lost you somewhere along the way.
Perhaps, when I turned that dark corner
and felt him lurking in my shadows,
knowing soon that he'll lay hold of me.

Please return to me once more.
Be my beacon of light as of old,
among stormy seas and uneasy souls.
Bring back that perfect peace
that I once felt so sincerely.

Simona Frosin
Full Marathon, Hour 24
Galati, Romania

Maybe

there's nothing more to be said—
humans sank in the seas of oblivion
maybe there is still hope
and empathy will prevail

maybe not everything is lost
and we are not doomed yet…
maybe we will all meet in the heart
of the rainbow after this big storm

Jillian Calahan
Full Marathon, Hour 24
Selah, WA, USA

Komorebi

How many times have I
lost sight of the sun?
My branching fears
layered thick with
the toil of mossy doubt.
The sky feels so strange,
like a breadth of ghosts.

I cannot see the clouds.
Their ethereal whispers float by,
lost to the darkness.
And so that fear grows—
Taller. Wi(l)der. Stronger,
choking me in its shadows.

But if I look closely,
through the brittle cracks
and narrow fissures,
light bleeds through,
tiny rays of promise
exploding out in all directions,

a reminder
that even in my darkest,
most haunting hours,
it only takes one band of hope,
to make my way back to the light.

SUNFLOWERS, LIGHT AND PRAYERS

Pauline Olthof-Youn
Half Marathon, Hour 5
Hamilton, ON

Sunflower

A sunflower field,
Yellow rings around black holes
Stargazing, breathing

Wendie Donabie
Half Marathon, Hour 11
Bracebridge, Ontario

Dawn's Kiss

The first rays of dawn
        tip-toe
                across the dew-dropped grass
                          and leap
                                  into my window,
    flit across the polished floor,
        slink over silken sheets,
                and kiss
                      my face.

I relish such mornings,
like fresh bread and honey,
soft to chew and sweet on the tongue.

Light delights me as it plays through the day,
changing the mood of each place it touches.

Deanna Ngai
Full Marathon, Hour 7
Airdrie, Alberta Canada

Soothing Flowers

Swinging in a sunflower field,
I close my eyes and feel the breeze.
The hum of bees fills the air
and set my soul at ease.

I let my thoughts flow freely,
swinging in a sunflower field.
I daydream about the summer sun
and feel my mind is healed.

With pleasant sounds around me,
I sway placidly in my seat.
Swinging in a sunflower field
I feel the sun's soothing heat.

I open up my eyes and smile,
look around, nothing concealed.
I get up, refreshed from my time
of swinging in a sunflower field.

Cristy Watson
Half Marathon, Hour 8
Calgary, Alberta

Before First Light

the bow of moonlight plays across the string
of shadows, bringing cynosure to the moment

a sweet rhythm to the melancholy dance
of eagles, soaring above the firmament

gliding on the dreams of the innocent
holding conference with the stars

until day breaks

Karen Jacobson Burwell
Half Marathon, Hour 11
New Haven, CT., United States

In My Woods

A tunnel formed by trees
surrounds the path into my woods,
so many shades of green.
Deeper into the woods,
the shade makes it seem so dark
but walking here breeds joy.
This is my private park—
dappled light dances
on bright and dark green leaves.
Then a butterfly comes by
and settles on my sleeve.
Too soon, away it flies…
In my woods, my park of green
in solitude, I pray,
thankful for all I see,
for all God gives each day.

d-a-foster
Half Marathon, Hour 7
North Vancouver, BC Canada

Flowers Bloom in Library Square

Flowers bloom in Library Square,
blossoms of red, white, purple, and gold.
People are sitting at tables and chairs,
visiting, talking, both young and old.

Steadfast the effort of gardening crews.
Flowers bloom in Library Square.
Above, white gulls soar in skies deep blue.
Peaceful it seems for all who are there.

But then comes a man, distracted, who stares
confused perhaps by high noon heat.
Flowers bloom in Library Square.
An older gentleman stands to his feet,

approaches the man and offers him aid—
some water, companions, comfort, a chair,
a safe place to sit in the cool of the shade
where flowers bloom in Library Square.

Nandiya Nyx
Full Marathon, Hour 5
Portland, Maine, United States

What's Left

Left
plucked
from the most fragrant flowers
my favorite flowers
denuded flowers.

Left
petals
the deepest purples, yellows tipped with orange
like an icy Fanta
on an August noon in Miami.

Left
in a heap
on the ugly desk chair, broken seat adjustment
draped with the jacket
that still smells of you.

This
is what's left—
freesia
        freesia
                freesia.

Mel Neet
Full Marathon, Hour 17
Kansas City, Missouri

There have been no Fireflies

I last saw a firefly when I was a child.
I remember a preponderance
of their flickering every summer.

Maybe because
I'm long past bartering
with my mother to stay outside
in the backyard,
I no longer have the vantage
from which to succumb
to their blinking presence.

Katie Scholan
Full Marathon, Hour 1
Bristol, UK

Nowhere

Lights in the city are hung from chains,
the quiet bound with voices.

We step between the shadowed parks,
blind spots in a panopticon where,
uncaught by luminescent breath,
we flee.

There is a bridge across the night
but it is garlanded with stars
to rob us of our twilight eyes.
Glittered reminiscence,
the sound of singing flows below
unseen.

The rearing land is lined with trees,
an all-embracing veil of black.
One lamp remains, the city's hand,
a toll booth guarding nowhere;
we leave the past behind unpaid
and free.

Lori Carlson
Half Marathon, Hour 9
Madison, NJ

Elk Eyes

I ripped the elbow of my jacket
on a broken lightbulb
hidden in a bucket
that smelled vaguely of cinnamon.
It was in that carport
down by the bayou,
where the mural of a dying elk,
blood the color of beets,
stares as if pleading with me,
in his death tremor,
to be set free.

Anjana Sen
Full Marathon, Hour 6
Glasgow, Scotland, UK

Conversations With God

It should have been the stuff of nightmarish fright;
the cavernous opening, an apocalyptic sight.
But strangely it wasn't, it felt just right,
as I stepped up to the very edge of the night,
to the very last ledge of light.
Below the beyond, it was bright—
it was white and white and white.

'Are you God,' I asked?
I knew this light; I lit it every day.
It's my little *Diya*, before I pray,
untensed. After my shower, cleansed.
I do nothing, say nothing,
till I pray for the day ahead.

'We meet every morning,' said the light.
Benign. Benevolent. Wonderous. White.

Shame floods my blood,
my prayers were nought but greed.
A flux of negotiations, wants and needs.

'You get the plumber to fix the leak today, God,
and I promise to write 2000 words.'
'You help me lose two more kilos, God,
and I'll cook from scratch everyday.'
And more recently,
'You make my Ma get better, God,
and I promise to give up Candy Crush forever.'

'Can we talk now, please God?'

I prayed. I thanked. We talked—

We talked, as the ground beneath me
swelled and curved and rolled back to Life.

Then, back to wakefulness.

Index of Poets

Adams, KV	11
Achoch, Mildred	45
Adegboro, Michelle	79
Agali, Ofuma	50
Albers, Cinthia	34
Andrew, Shaughnessy	91
Aôndona, Daniel	75
April Soliman, Ayah	95
Balliro, Lenore	28
Banerjee, Ipsita	66
Bostelman, Amy	82
Bruce Patterson, David	22
Burwell, Karen Jacobson	105
Call, Karen B.	62
Calahan, Jillian	97
Carmony, Diane	70
Carlson, Lori	110
Chukwuma-Eke, Pacella	35
Crabtree, Amber L.	81
Curnow, Daryl	65
Darlington, Marci	58
Donabie, Wendie	102
Duncan, Sandra	84
Durr, Shirley	16
Dwivedi, Bhasha	78
Ekawu, Elizabeth Imaji	24
Eckler, Jo	60
Elaine Smith, Evelyn	20
Flores, Mary Eugene	76
Foster, d-a	106
Frosin, Simona	96
Gerber, Pamela	59
Gildersleeve, Britton	56
Gogo, Tanya	57
Grant, Daphne Joy	51
Gopalakrishnan Prakash	14
Hasson, Brian	36
Herndon, Cindy	21
Hernandez, Cynthia	87
HighEarth8888 (MardiosaYanes)	93
Humeston, Dart	55
Hutcheson, Stefanie	68
Imelda Maguire	43

Isa Yahaya, Sa'ada	17
Johnson, Sandra	31
Kalarickal, Sangita	23
Karanam, Aarthi V.	67
Katzive, Bonnie	72
Knizhnik, Erica	47
Leonard, Leroy	63
Maguire, Imelda	43
Markowitz, Anna	94
McNicholas, Kate	19
Moinet, Katrina	77
Montgomery-Hughes, Lee	46
Neet, Mel	108
Ngai, Deanna	103
Nyx, Nandiya	107
O'Neill, Diane	48
Olthof-Youn, Pauline	101
Pavrey, Renata	41
Potter, Amanda	27
Prost, Carol	12
Riofrio, Maria	92
Ross, Stephanie	49
Salmon, Pamela	71
Sankar, Shloka	29
Scholan, Katie	109
Sen, Anjana	111
Shankar, Vidya	39
Smith, Evelyn Elaine	20
Sollinger Walker, Ellen	15
Spadoni, Tim	80
Storts, Sue	52
Stomska, Katarzyna	85
Sousa, Liane	83
Steinshouer, Betty Jean	40
Storts, Sue	52
Schwartz, Harvey	44
Umbrino, Philip	13
Varadharajan, Namratha	18
Wahl, Margarette	86
Walker, Ellen Sollinger	15
Watson, Cristy	104
Wells, Diana Kristine	42
Willsen, Kell	33
Wilson, David L.	64
Yahaya, Sa'ada Isa	17
Yañez (HighEarth8888), Mardiosa	93

www.ingramcontent.com/pod-product-compliance
Lightning Source LLC
Chambersburg PA
CBHW060534080526
44586CB00012B/724